# Bear Spotting

Written by Isabel Thomas

## Contents



Collins

# Look out!

There are bears about.
Each kind of bear has:

- a long snout
- small ears
- a short tail.

But bears are found in different habitats, and eat different foods.

# Brown bear

This group of brown bears is fishing in Alaska. They stand on boulders in the river and wait for fish to jump into their mouths!

# Panda

Wild pandas are found in China, where they eat just one plant: bamboo. Their paws have an extra bone to grasp bamboo shoots and stems.

# Polar bear

Polar bears are good at swimming. They roam the cold Arctic, hunting seals, reindeer and sea birds.

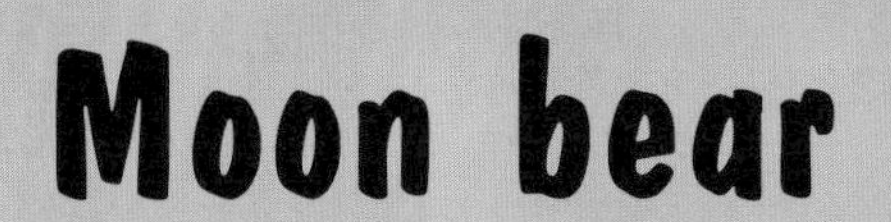

# Moon bear

Moon bears
can be found in China,
Japan and
the Himalayas.
They munch nuts,
seeds, insects, birds
and rodents.

# Sloth bear

Sloth bears hang upside down from trees. Their front teeth are missing so they can suck up insects. Their nostrils seal shut to stop termites crawling in!

# Sun bear

The world's smallest bear, the sun bear, hides in rainforests. Sharp claws help it tear open beehives and its strong jaws can crack coconuts!

# American black bear

In North America, black bears visit meadows to eat grass and other plants. They have been caught eating scraps that humans throw away, too.

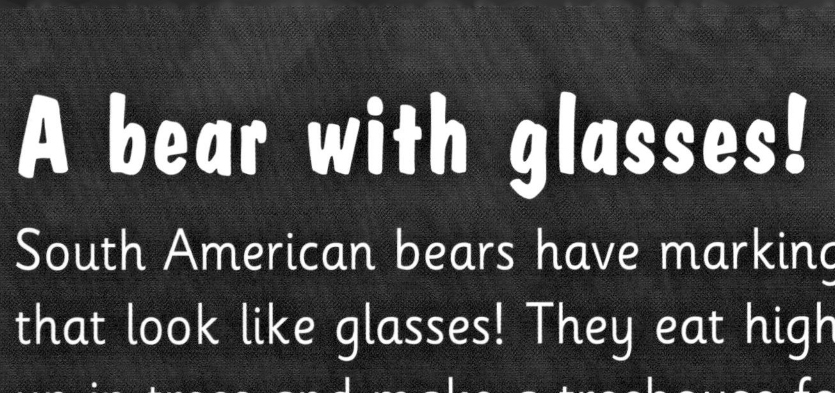

# A bear with glasses!

South American bears have markings that look like glasses! They eat high up in trees and make a treehouse for sleeping in.

# Under threat

Six of the bears in this book are rare and under threat. We can help bears by protecting their homes.

# Spotting bears

# After reading

**Letters and Sounds:** Phase 5

**Word count:** 259

**Focus phonemes:** /ai/ ay, ei, ey, a-e /igh/ i, i-e /oa/ o, ow, ol, o-e /oo/ u, ou /ee/ ea /ow/ ou /ar/ a /or/ augh, aw, al /air/ ear, are, ere /ur/ ir, or /ear/ eer /e/ ea /u/ o

**Common exception words:** of, to, the, into, by, are, we, be, have, so, one, where, house, their

**Curriculum links:** Science: Animals, including humans

**National Curriculum learning objectives:** Spoken language: articulate and justify answers, arguments and opinions; Reading/Word reading: apply phonic knowledge and skills as the route to decode words, read accurately by blending sounds in unfamiliar words containing GPCs that have been taught, read other words of more than one syllable that contain taught GPCs, read aloud accurately books that are consistent with their developing phonic knowledge; Reading/Comprehension: understand both the books they can already read accurately and fluently ... by: drawing on what they already know or on background information and vocabulary provided by the teacher

## Developing fluency

- Your child may enjoy hearing you read the book. Model reading with lots of expression.
- You may wish to take turns to read a page.

## Phonic practise

- Look at page 2 together and turn to the first sentence. Ask your child:
    - Can you find two words that rhyme? (*bear*, *there*)
    - For each word, can you point to the part of the word that represents the /air/ sound?
    - Can you think of other words that contain the /air/ sound? (e.g. *hair*, *care*, *pear*)
- You could now do the same thing for the /ow/ sound on page 4 (*brown*, *mouths*) or the /ee/ sound on page 18 (*sleeping*, *eats*, *trees*).